STAMPED

stamp lovers yearly planner

Name: _____   In case of emergency, kindly contact:

Email Address: _____   Name: _____

Contact Number: _____   Relationship: _____

Birthday: _____   Contact Details: _____

MY NOTES

MY NOTES

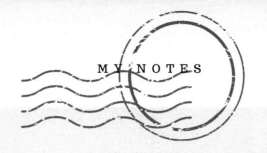
MY NOTES

Monthly Planner

Note:

1	2

3	4	5	6	7
8	9	10	11	12
13	14	15	16	17
18	19	20	21	22
23	24	25	26	27
28	29	30	31	

Monthly Planner

Note:

				1	2
3	4	5	6	7	
8	9	10	11	12	
13	14	15	16	17	
18	19	20	21	22	
23	24	25	26	27	
28	29	30	31		

Monthly Planner

Note:

1	2

3	4	5	6	7
8	9	10	11	12
13	14	15	16	17
18	19	20	21	22
23	24	25	26	27
28	29	30	31	

Monthly Planner

Note:

				1	2
3	4	5	6	7	
8	9	10	11	12	
13	14	15	16	17	
18	19	20	21	22	
23	24	25	26	27	
28	29	30	31		

Monthly Planner

Note:

			1	2
3	4	5	6	7
8	9	10	11	12
13	14	15	16	17
18	19	20	21	22
23	24	25	26	27
28	29	30	31	

Monthly Planner

Note:

			1	2
3	4	5	6	7
8	9	10	11	12
13	14	15	16	17
18	19	20	21	22
23	24	25	26	27
28	29	30	31	

Monthly Planner

Note:

1	2

3	4	5	6	7
8	9	10	11	12
13	14	15	16	17
18	19	20	21	22
23	24	25	26	27
28	29	30	31	

Monthly Planner

Note:

			1	2
3	4	5	6	7
8	9	10	11	12
13	14	15	16	17
18	19	20	21	22
23	24	25	26	27
28	29	30	31	

Monthly Planner

Note:

1	2

3	4	5	6	7
8	9	10	11	12
13	14	15	16	17
18	19	20	21	22
23	24	25	26	27
28	29	30	31	

Monthly Planner

Note:

			1	2
3	4	5	6	7
8	9	10	11	12
13	14	15	16	17
18	19	20	21	22
23	24	25	26	27
28	29	30	31	

Monthly Planner

Note:

				1	2
3	4	5	6	7	
8	9	10	11	12	
13	14	15	16	17	
18	19	20	21	22	
23	24	25	26	27	
28	29	30	31		

Monthly Planner

Note:

			1	2
3	4	5	6	7
8	9	10	11	12
13	14	15	16	17
18	19	20	21	22
23	24	25	26	27
28	29	30	31	

WEEKLY SCHEDULE PLANNER

MONTH

WEEK NO.

MONDAY

TUESDAY

WEDNESDAY

THURSDAY

FRIDAY

SATURDAY

SUNDAY

NOTES

WEEKLY SCHEDULE PLANNER

MONTH

WEEK NO.

MONDAY

TUESDAY

WEDNESDAY

THURSDAY

FRIDAY

SATURDAY

SUNDAY

NOTES

WEEKLY
SCHEDULE
PLANNER

MONTH

WEEK NO.

MONDAY

TUESDAY

WEDNESDAY

THURSDAY

FRIDAY

SATURDAY

SUNDAY

NOTES

WEEKLY SCHEDULE PLANNER

MONTH

WEEK NO.

MONDAY

TUESDAY

WEDNESDAY

THURSDAY

FRIDAY

SATURDAY

SUNDAY

NOTES

80-GODIŠNJICA PROPASTI TITANIKA

JUGOSLAVIJA

PTT

R. BOJANIĆ

1992

150

FORUM

EEKLY
CHEDULE
LANNER

MONTH

VEEK NO.

MONDAY

TUESDAY

WEDNESDAY

THURSDAY

FRIDAY

SATURDAY

SUNDAY

NOTES

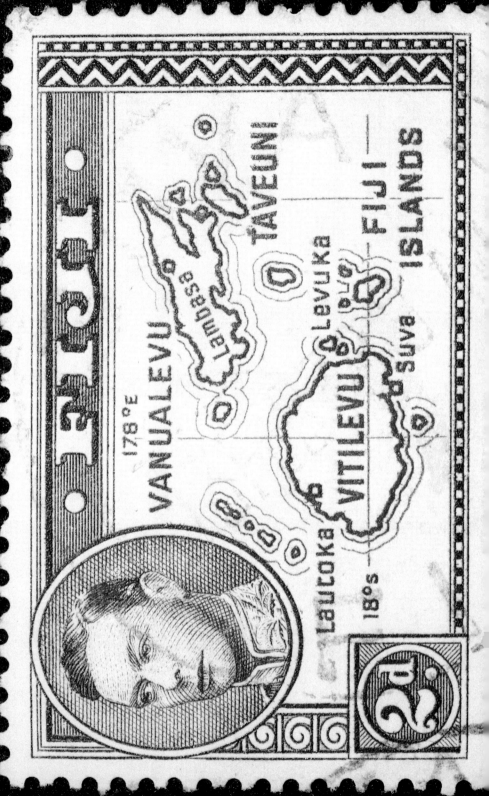

WEEKLY SCHEDULE PLANNER

MONTH

WEEK NO.

MONDAY	TUESDAY

WEDNESDAY	THURSDAY	FRIDAY

SATURDAY	SUNDAY	NOTES

WEEKLY SCHEDULE PLANNER

MONTH

WEEK NO.

MONDAY

TUESDAY

WEDNESDAY

THURSDAY

FRIDAY

SATURDAY

SUNDAY

NOTES

REPUBLIQUE FRANCAISE

18 F

POSTES

BEYNAC · CAZENAC (Dordogne) MASELIN

EEKLY CHEDULE LANNER

MONTH

WEEK NO.

MONDAY

TUESDAY

WEDNESDAY

THURSDAY

FRIDAY

SATURDAY

SUNDAY

NOTES

REPUBLIQUE FRANÇAISE

Postes PARIS 030

WEEKLY SCHEDULE PLANNER

MONTH

WEEK NO.

MONDAY

TUESDAY

WEDNESDAY

THURSDAY

FRIDAY

SATURDAY

SUNDAY

NOTES

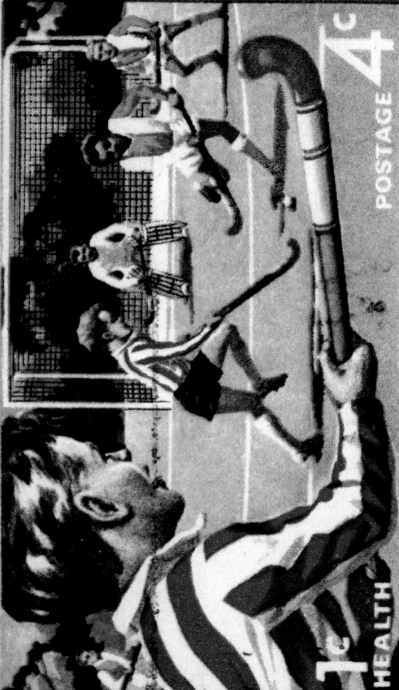

EEKLY CHEDULE LANNER

MONTH

VEEK NO.

MONDAY

TUESDAY

WEDNESDAY

THURSDAY

FRIDAY

SATURDAY

SUNDAY

NOTES

70 ЛЕТ СО ДНЯ РОЖДЕНИЯ·

ПОЧТА СССР · 1963

4 к.

В. Маяковский

WEEKLY SCHEDULE PLANNER

MONTH

WEEK NO.

MONDAY

TUESDAY

WEDNESDAY

THURSDAY

FRIDAY

SATURDAY

SUNDAY

NOTES

POSTES
LAO

1983

2ᵏ

EEKLY
CHEDULE
LANNER

MONTH

WEEK NO.

MONDAY

TUESDAY

WEDNESDAY

THURSDAY

FRIDAY

SATURDAY

SUNDAY

NOTES

WEEKLY SCHEDULE PLANNER

MONTH

WEEK NO.

MONDAY

TUESDAY

WEDNESDAY

THURSDAY

FRIDAY

SATURDAY

SUNDAY

NOTES

WEEKLY SCHEDULE PLANNER

MONTH

WEEK NO.

MONDAY

TUESDAY

WEDNESDAY

THURSDAY

FRIDAY

SATURDAY

SUNDAY

NOTES

МУЗЕЙ В.И.ЛЕНИНА
В ЛЕЙПЦИГЕ
1986
LENIN-GEDENKSTÄTTE
5 ПОЧТА СССР

EEKLY
CHEDULE
LANNER

MONTH

WEEK NO.

MONDAY	TUESDAY

WEDNESDAY	THURSDAY	FRIDAY

SATURDAY	SUNDAY	NOTES

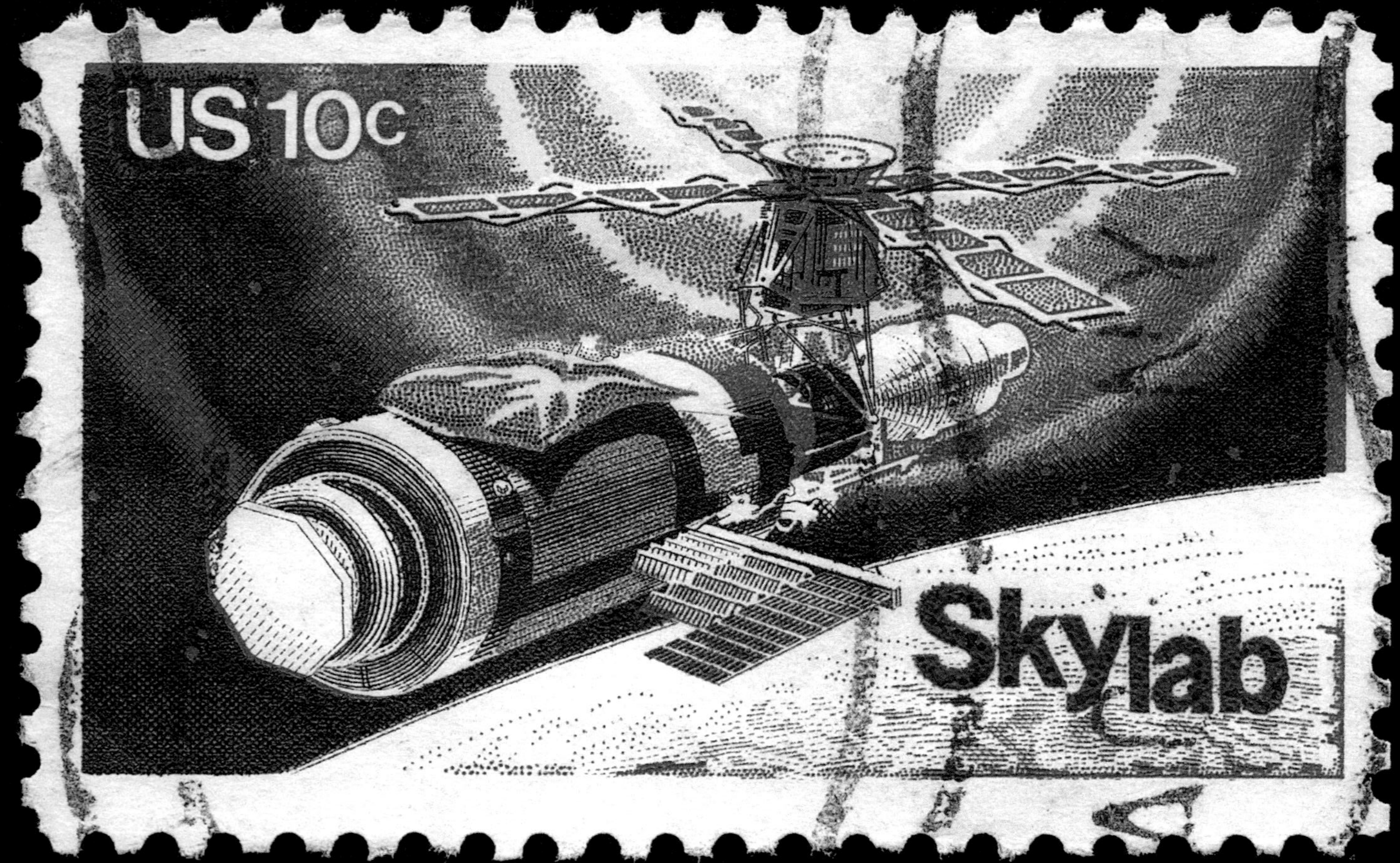
US 10c
Skylab

EEKLY CHEDULE LANNER

MONTH

WEEK NO.

MONDAY

TUESDAY

WEDNESDAY

THURSDAY

FRIDAY

SATURDAY

SUNDAY

NOTES

EEKLY
CHEDULE
LANNER

MONTH

VEEK NO.

MONDAY

TUESDAY

WEDNESDAY

THURSDAY

FRIDAY

SATURDAY

SUNDAY

NOTES

UNITED STATES

6¢

WATERFOWL CONSERVATION

EEKLY CHEDULE LANNER

MONTH

VEEK NO.

MONDAY

TUESDAY

WEDNESDAY

THURSDAY

FRIDAY

SATURDAY

SUNDAY

NOTES

EEKLY
CHEDULE
LANNER

MONTH

WEEK NO.

MONDAY

TUESDAY

WEDNESDAY

THURSDAY

FRIDAY

SATURDAY

SUNDAY

NOTES

EEKLY CHEDULE LANNER

MONTH

VEEK NO.

MONDAY	TUESDAY

WEDNESDAY	THURSDAY	FRIDAY

SATURDAY	SUNDAY	NOTES

EEKLY
CHEDULE
LANNER

MONTH

VEEK NO.

MONDAY

TUESDAY

WEDNESDAY

THURSDAY

FRIDAY

SATURDAY

SUNDAY

NOTES

EEKLY CHEDULE LANNER

MONTH

WEEK NO.

MONDAY

TUESDAY

WEDNESDAY

THURSDAY

FRIDAY

SATURDAY

SUNDAY

NOTES

EEKLY
CHEDULE
LANNER

MONTH

VEEK NO.

MONDAY

TUESDAY

WEDNESDAY

THURSDAY

FRIDAY

SATURDAY

SUNDAY

NOTES

EEKLY
CHEDULE
LANNER

MONTH

WEEK NO.

MONDAY

TUESDAY

WEDNESDAY

THURSDAY

FRIDAY

SATURDAY

SUNDAY

NOTES

EEKLY
CHEDULE
LANNER

MONTH

WEEK NO.

MONDAY

TUESDAY

WEDNESDAY

THURSDAY

FRIDAY

SATURDAY

SUNDAY

NOTES

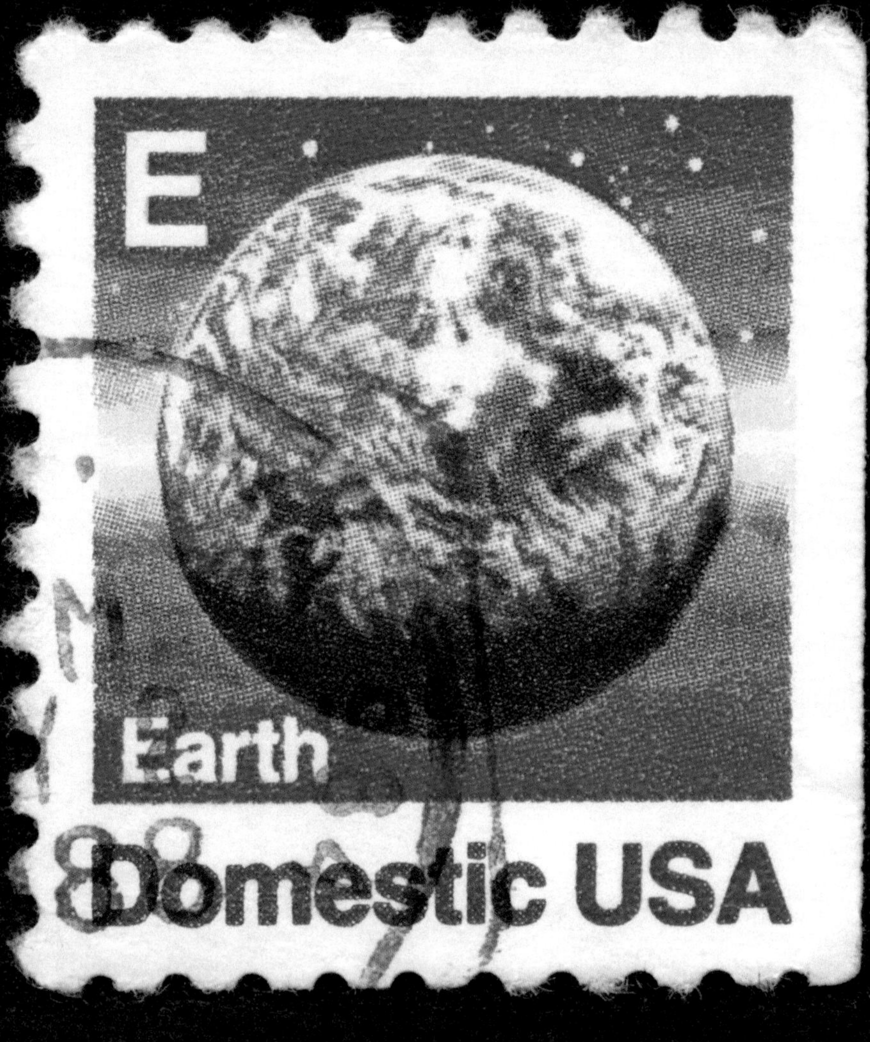
E
Earth
Domestic USA

EEKLY
CHEDULE
LANNER

MONTH

WEEK NO.

MONDAY

TUESDAY

WEDNESDAY

THURSDAY

FRIDAY

SATURDAY

SUNDAY

NOTES

EEKLY
CHEDULE
LANNER

MONTH

VEEK NO.

MONDAY	TUESDAY

WEDNESDAY	THURSDAY	FRIDAY

SATURDAY	SUNDAY	NOTES

EEKLY
CHEDULE
LANNER

MONTH

WEEK NO.

MONDAY

TUESDAY

WEDNESDAY

THURSDAY

FRIDAY

SATURDAY

SUNDAY

NOTES

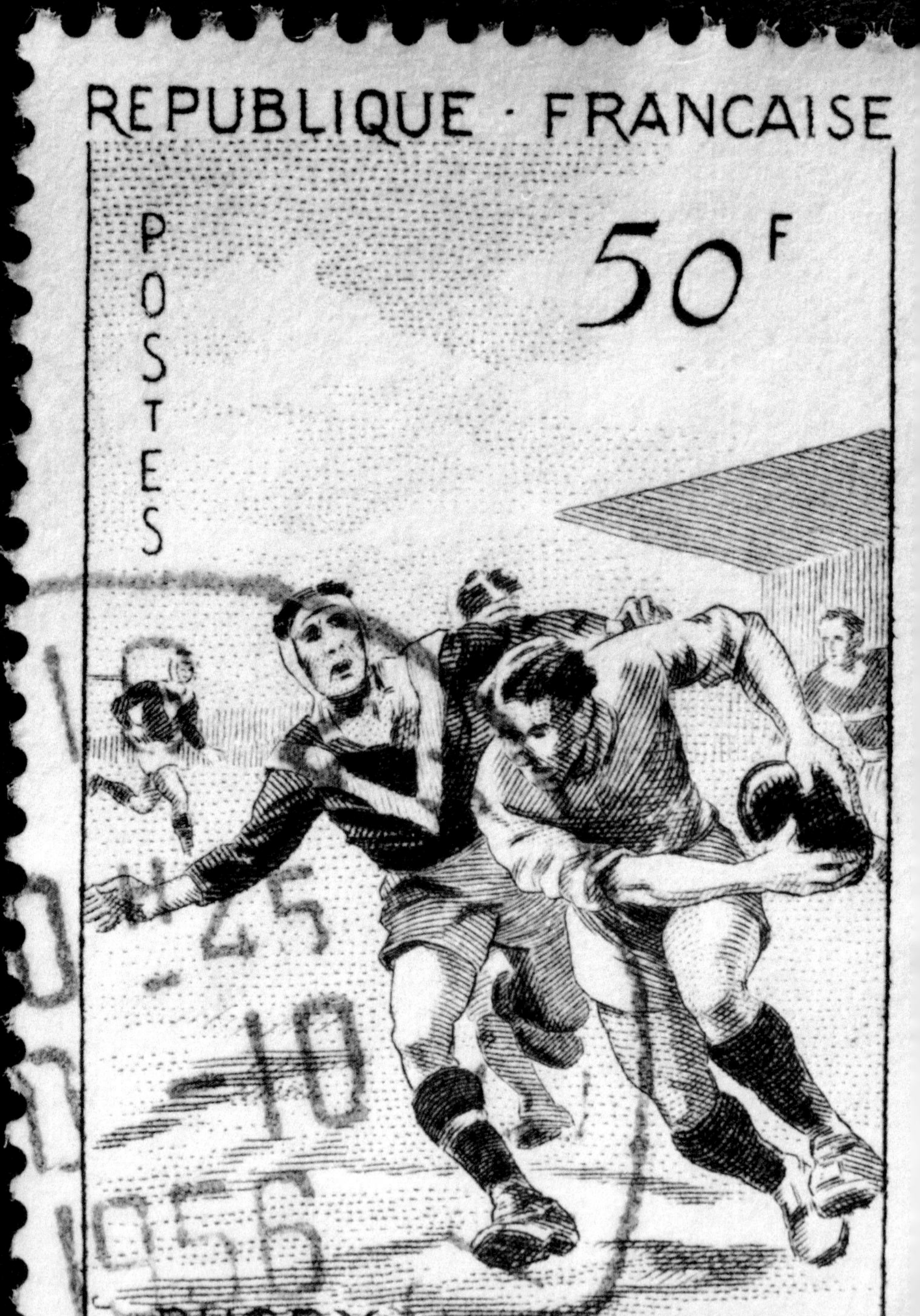
REPUBLIQUE · FRANCAISE
POSTES
50F
RUGBY
J. PIEL
R. SERRES

EEKLY
CHEDULE
LANNER

MONTH

WEEK NO.

MONDAY

TUESDAY

WEDNESDAY

THURSDAY

FRIDAY

SATURDAY

SUNDAY

NOTES

ГОСУДАРСТВЕННЫЙ ЭРМИТАЖ

· ФЕТТИ · ПОРТРЕТ АКТЕРА ·

1982 ПОЧТА СССР

EEKLY
CHEDULE
LANNER

MONTH

WEEK NO.

MONDAY

TUESDAY

WEDNESDAY

THURSDAY

FRIDAY

SATURDAY

SUNDAY

NOTES

30 f.

HARMINCZ FILLÉR.

1898

EEKLY
CHEDULE
LANNER

MONTH

VEEK NO.

MONDAY

TUESDAY

WEDNESDAY

THURSDAY

FRIDAY

SATURDAY

SUNDAY

NOTES

EEKLY
CHEDULE
LANNER

MONTH

VEEK NO.

MONDAY	TUESDAY

WEDNESDAY	THURSDAY	FRIDAY

SATURDAY	SUNDAY	NOTES

EEKLY
CHEDULE
LANNER

MONTH

VEEK NO.

MONDAY

TUESDAY

WEDNESDAY

THURSDAY

FRIDAY

SATURDAY

SUNDAY

NOTES

WEEKLY SCHEDULE PLANNER

MONTH

WEEK NO.

MONDAY

TUESDAY

WEDNESDAY

THURSDAY

FRIDAY

SATURDAY

SUNDAY

NOTES

EEKLY
CHEDULE
LANNER

MONTH

WEEK NO.

MONDAY

TUESDAY

WEDNESDAY

THURSDAY

FRIDAY

SATURDAY

SUNDAY

NOTES

EEKLY
CHEDULE
LANNER

MONTH

WEEK NO.

MONDAY	TUESDAY

WEDNESDAY	THURSDAY	FRIDAY

SATURDAY	SUNDAY	NOTES

アホウドリ
Diomedea albatrus

20

自然保護

日本郵便 NIPPON

EEKLY
CHEDULE
LANNER

MONTH

VEEK NO.

MONDAY	TUESDAY

WEDNESDAY	THURSDAY	FRIDAY

SATURDAY	SUNDAY	NOTES

AUSTRALIA 22c

White Tailed Kingfisher

EEKLY CHEDULE LANNER

MONTH

WEEK NO.

MONDAY	TUESDAY

WEDNESDAY	THURSDAY	FRIDAY

SATURDAY	SUNDAY	NOTES

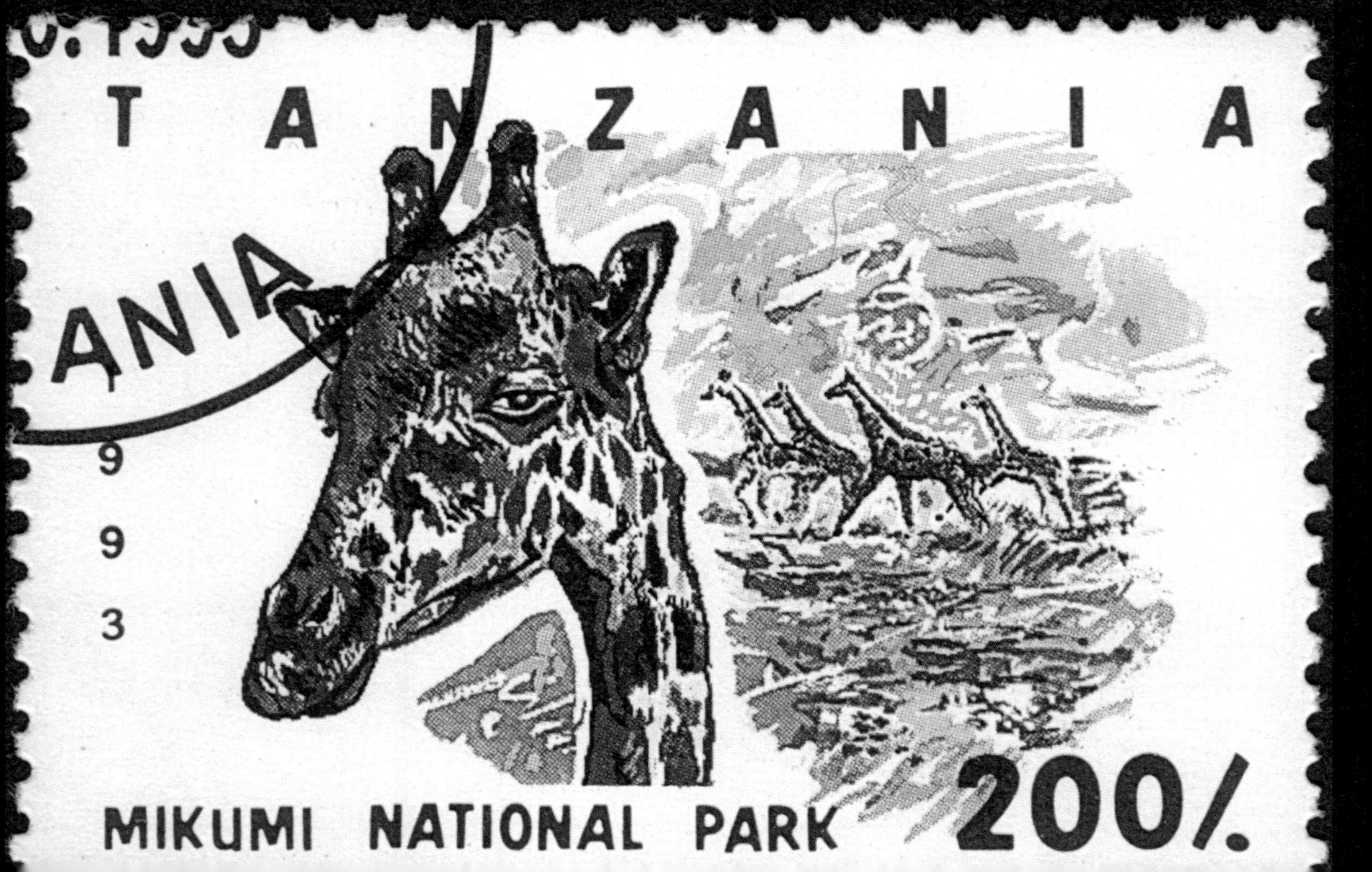
TANZANIA
1993
MIKUMI NATIONAL PARK
200/.

EEKLY
CHEDULE
LANNER

MONTH

WEEK NO.

MONDAY

TUESDAY

WEDNESDAY

THURSDAY

FRIDAY

SATURDAY

SUNDAY

NOTES

EEKLY
CHEDULE
LANNER

MONTH

VEEK NO.

MONDAY

TUESDAY

WEDNESDAY

THURSDAY

FRIDAY

SATURDAY

SUNDAY

NOTES

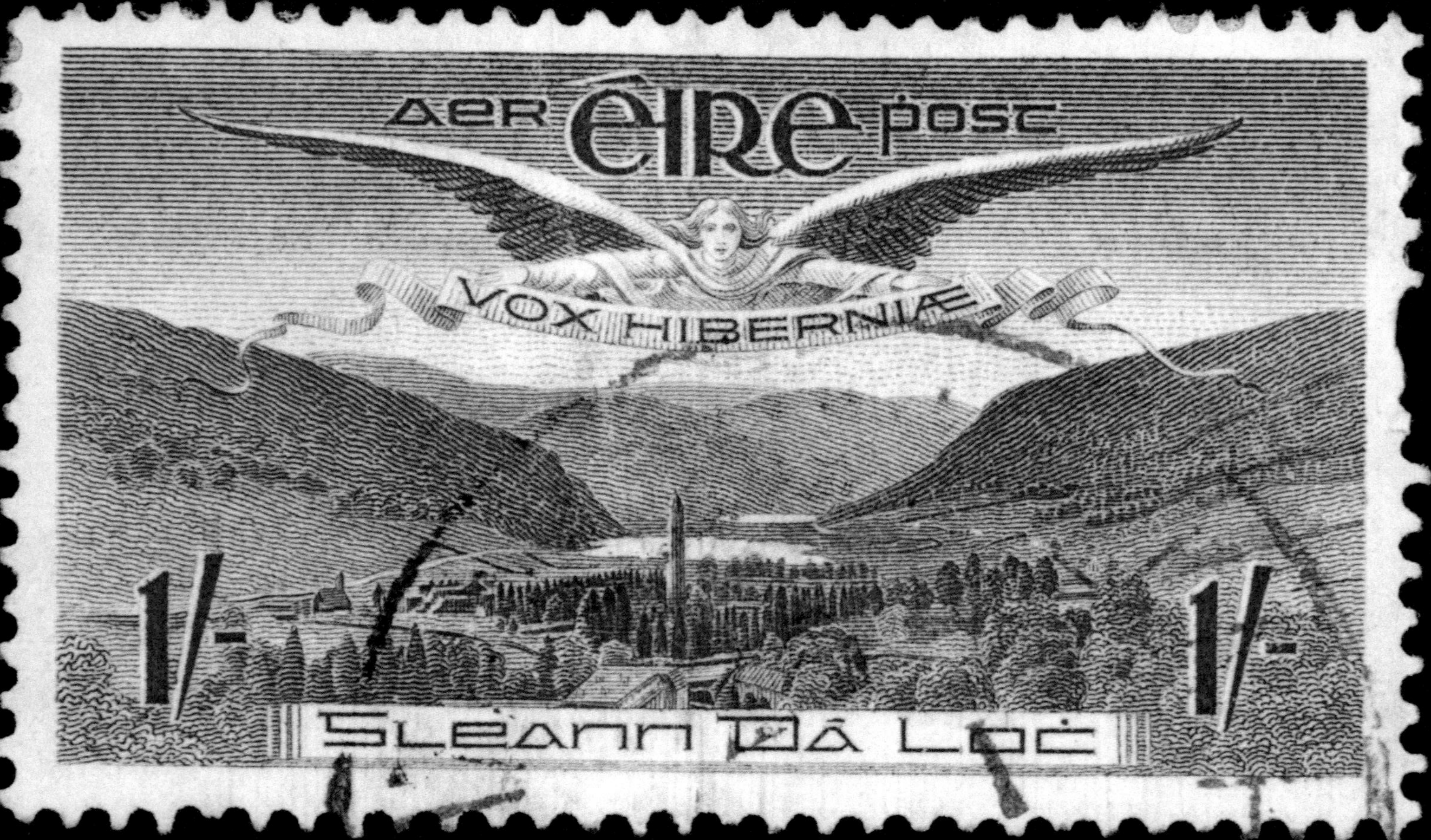

AER ÉIRE POST
VOX HIBERNIÆ
1/-
1/-
Gleann Dá Loċ

EEKLY
CHEDULE
LANNER

MONTH

VEEK NO.

MONDAY

TUESDAY

WEDNESDAY

THURSDAY

FRIDAY

SATURDAY

SUNDAY

NOTES

EEKLY CHEDULE LANNER

MONTH

WEEK NO.

MONDAY

TUESDAY

WEDNESDAY

THURSDAY

FRIDAY

SATURDAY

SUNDAY

NOTES

EEKLY
CHEDULE
LANNER

MONTH

WEEK NO.

MONDAY

TUESDAY

WEDNESDAY

THURSDAY

FRIDAY

SATURDAY

SUNDAY

NOTES

CEPT

Europa

NEDERLAND

25 c

EEKLY
CHEDULE
LANNER

MONTH

VEEK NO.

MONDAY

TUESDAY

WEDNESDAY

THURSDAY

FRIDAY

SATURDAY

SUNDAY

NOTES

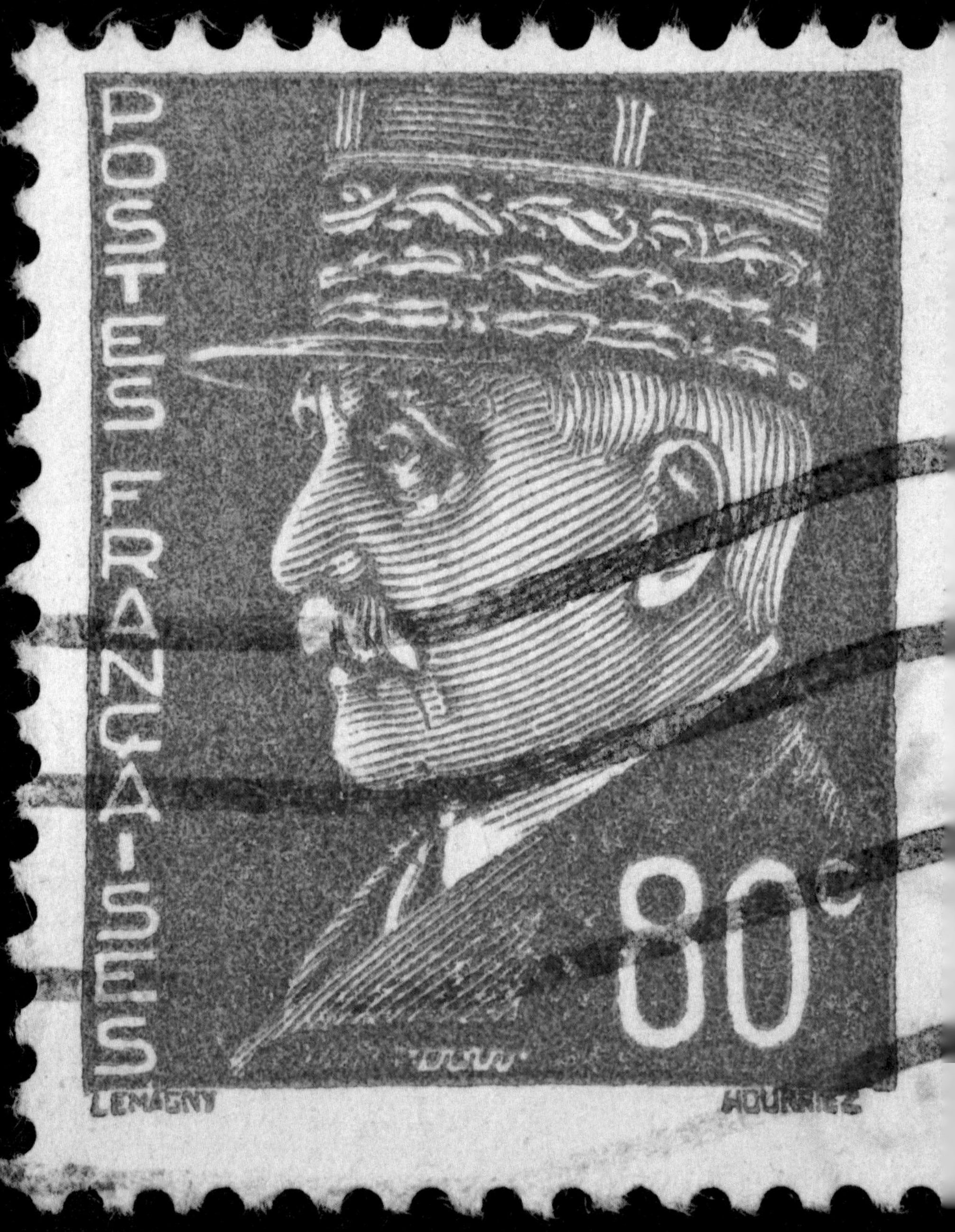
POSTES FRANÇAISES
80c
LEMAGNY

EEKLY
CHEDULE
LANNER

MONTH

VEEK NO.

MONDAY

TUESDAY

WEDNESDAY

THURSDAY

FRIDAY

SATURDAY

SUNDAY

NOTES

POSTES FRANCE
ANNÉE
INTERNATIONALE
DE LA FEMME
1975 • 1.20

WEEKLY SCHEDULE PLANNER

MONTH

WEEK NO.

MONDAY

TUESDAY

WEDNESDAY

THURSDAY

FRIDAY

SATURDAY

SUNDAY

NOTES

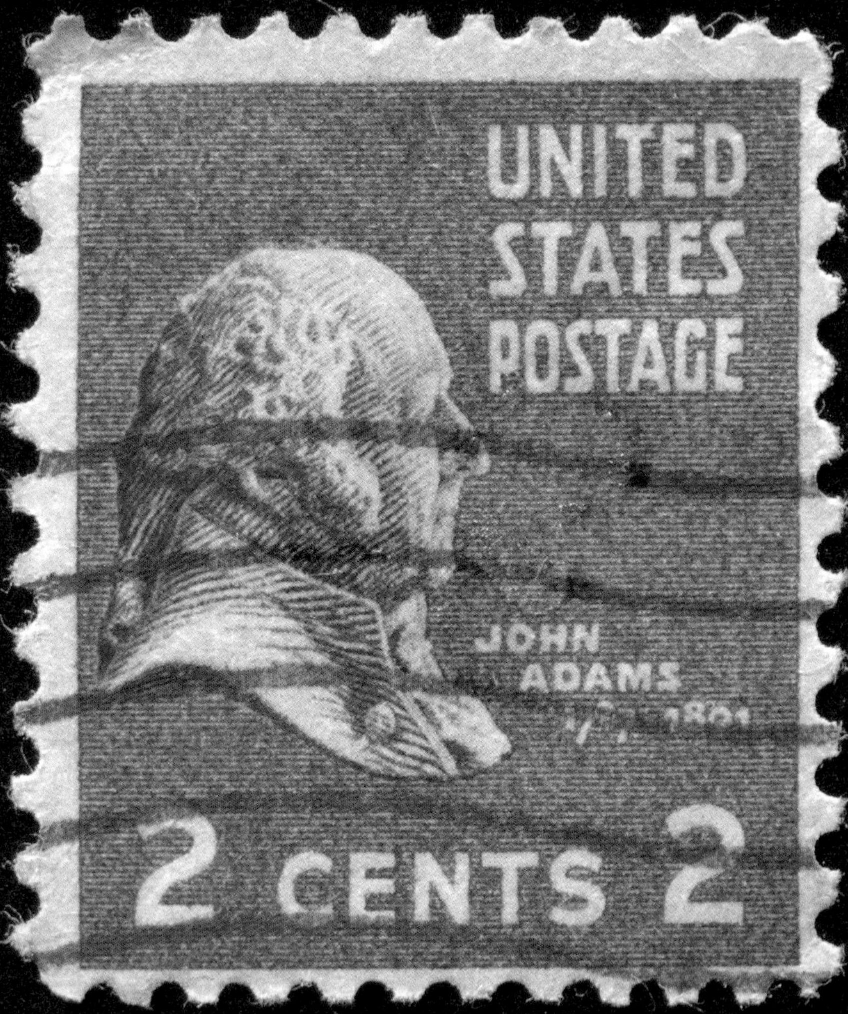
UNITED
STATES
POSTAGE
JOHN
ADAMS
2 CENTS 2

EEKLY
CHEDULE
LANNER

MONTH

VEEK NO.

MONDAY

TUESDAY

WEDNESDAY

THURSDAY

FRIDAY

SATURDAY

SUNDAY

NOTES

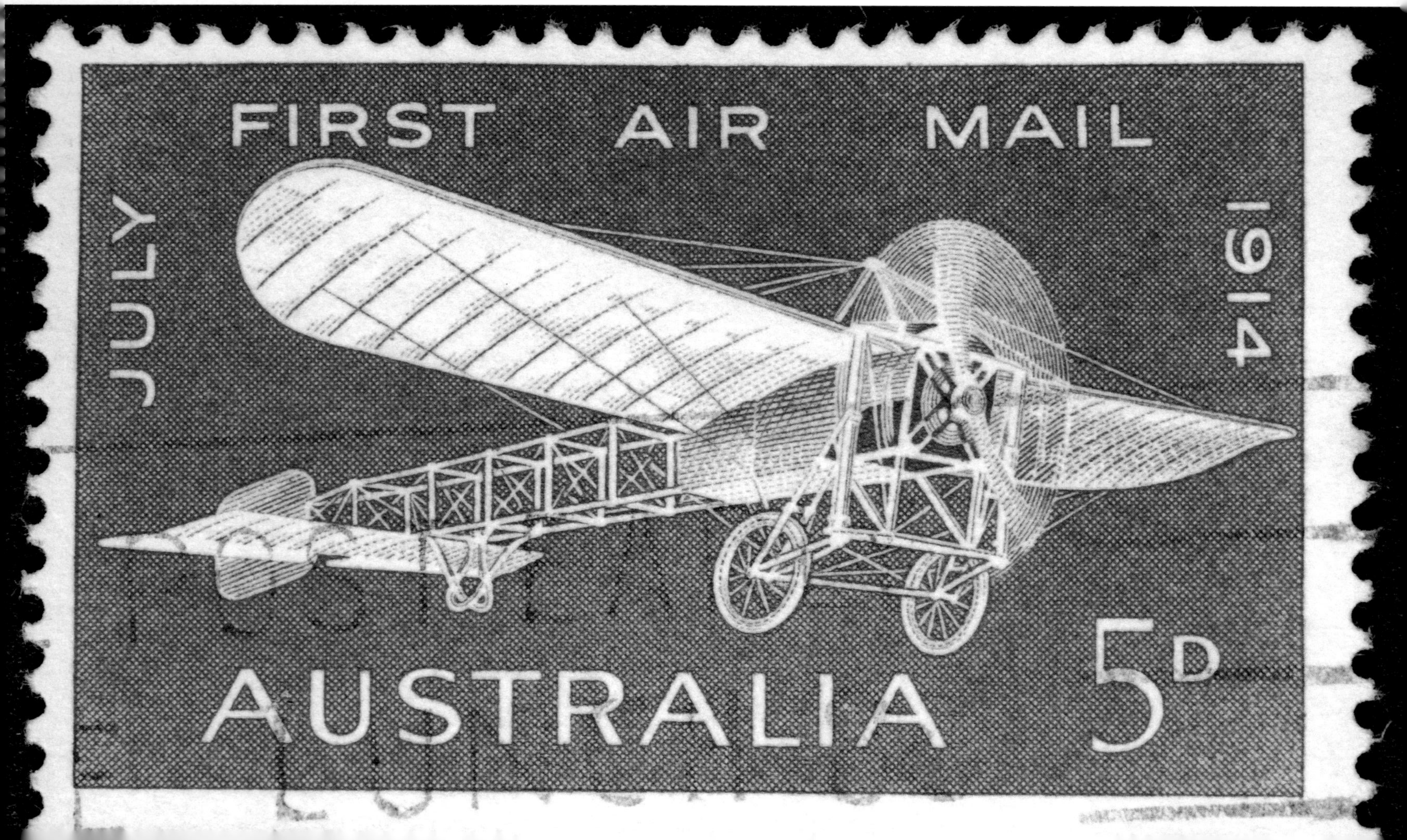
FIRST AIR MAIL
JULY
1914
AUSTRALIA
5D

WEEKLY SCHEDULE PLANNER

MONTH

WEEK NO.

MONDAY	TUESDAY

WEDNESDAY	THURSDAY	FRIDAY

SATURDAY	SUNDAY	NOTES

WEEKLY SCHEDULE PLANNER

MONTH

WEEK NO.

MONDAY

TUESDAY

WEDNESDAY

THURSDAY

FRIDAY

SATURDAY

SUNDAY

NOTES

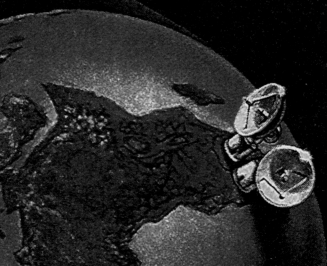

RSA 15c

Satellietkommunikasie. Satellite Communication.

Johan Hoekstra '75

EEKLY
CHEDULE
LANNER

MONTH

WEEK NO.

MONDAY

TUESDAY

WEDNESDAY

THURSDAY

FRIDAY

SATURDAY

SUNDAY

NOTES

CHINA

2元

中国邮政

开封祐国寺塔

1994—21

(4—4)T

WEEKLY SCHEDULE PLANNER

MONTH

WEEK NO.

MONDAY

TUESDAY

WEDNESDAY

THURSDAY

FRIDAY

SATURDAY

SUNDAY

NOTES

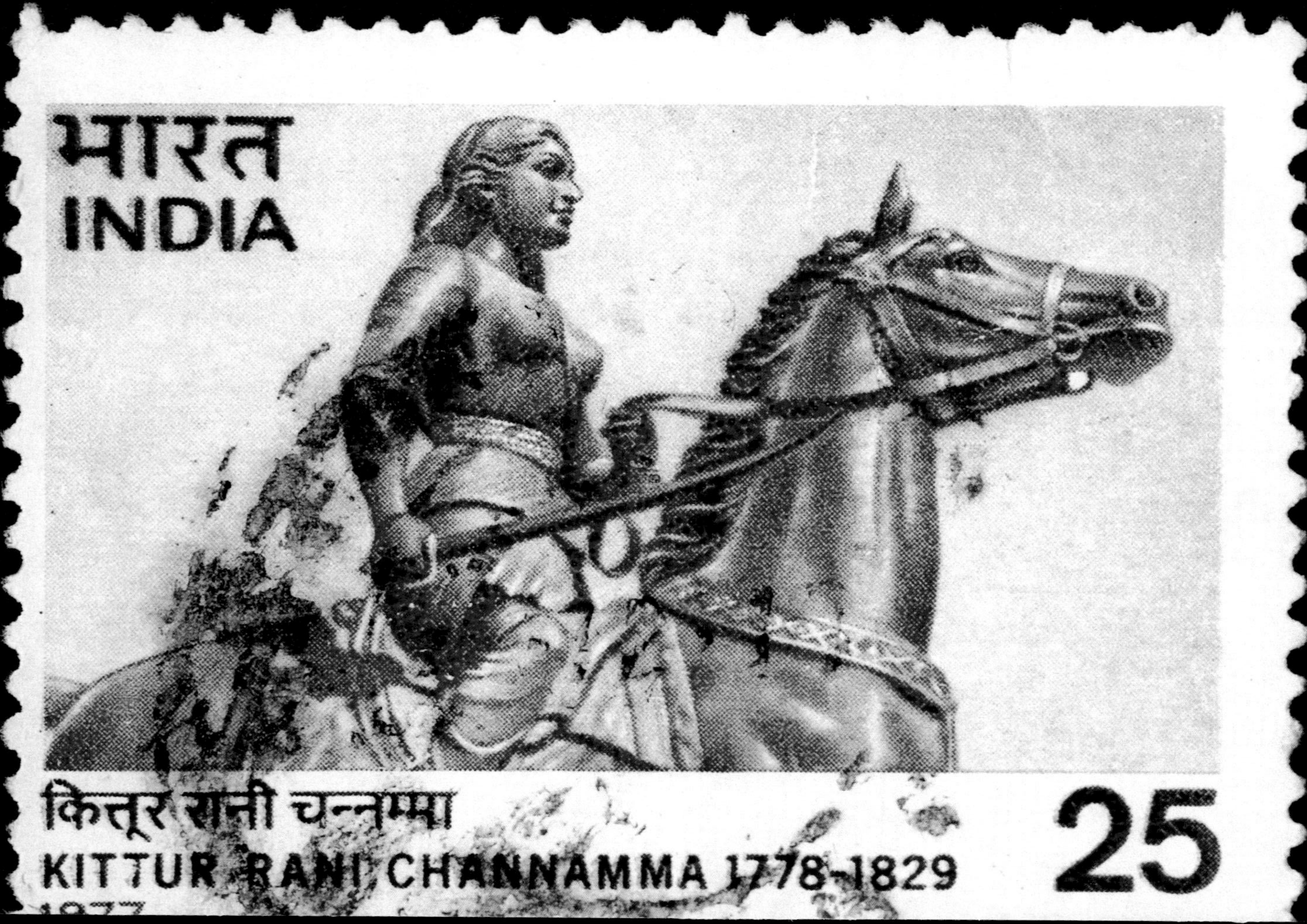
भारत
INDIA
कित्तूर रानी चन्नम्मा
KITTUR RANI CHANNAMMA 1778-1829
25

WEEKLY
SCHEDULE
PLANNER

MONTH

WEEK NO.

MONDAY	TUESDAY

WEDNESDAY	THURSDAY	FRIDAY

SATURDAY	SUNDAY	NOTES

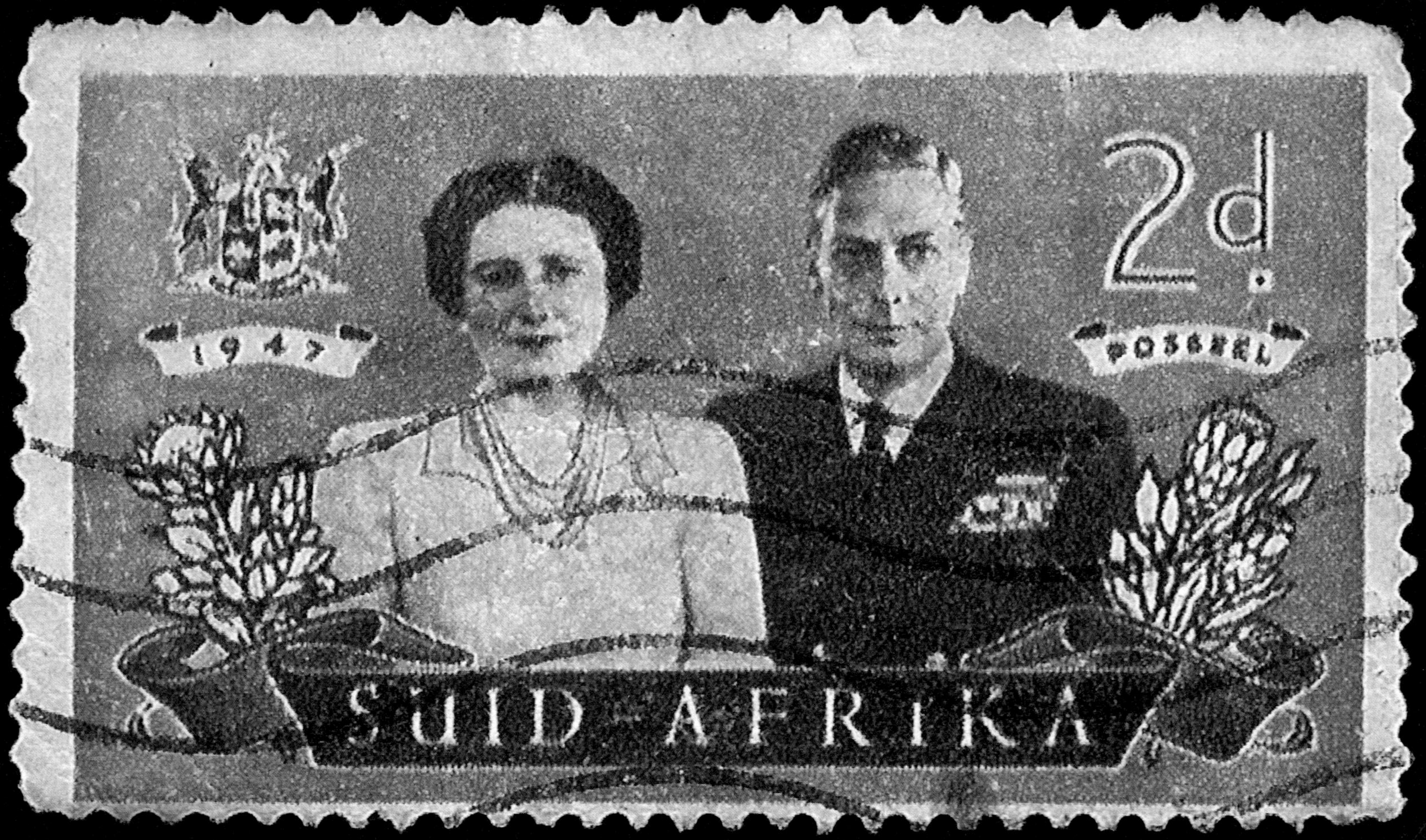

2d
1947
POSSEEL
SUID-AFRIKA